MW00999801

A Kalmus Classic Edition

HENRI

# BERTINI

## FORTY-NINE ETUDES

Opus 101 and 166

FOR PIANO

K 02043

Kalmus

# CONTENTS

Etude No. 1 in C Major .....5
Etude No. 2 in C Major .....6
Etude No. 3 in G Major .....7
Etude No. 4 in C Major .....8
Etude No. 5 in C Major .....9
Etude No. 6 in G Major .....10
Etude No. 7 in G Major .....11
Etude No. 8 in G Major .....12
Etude No. 9 in A Minor .....13
Etude No. 10 in G Major .....14
Etude No. 11 in D Major .....15
Etude No. 12 in F Major .....16
Etude No. 13 in C Major .....17
Etude No. 14 in A Major .....18
Etude No. 15 in C Major .....20
Etude No. 16 in B flat Major .....22
Etude No. 17 in C Major .....24
Etude No. 18 in E Minor .....25
Etude No. 19 in D Major .....26
Etude No. 20 in C Minor .....27
Etude No. 21 in D Major .....28
Etude No. 22 in E Minor .....29
Etude No. 23 in C Major .....30
Etude No. 24 in C Major .....31
Etude No. 25 in E flat Major .....32
Valse in B flat Major .....34
Canzonetta in A Minor .....36
Rondino in F Major .....38
Aria in A Major .....40
Minuet and Trio in E Minor .....42
Theme and Variations in E Minor .....43
Ballade in F Minor .....45
Marche in A Major .....46
Adagio in F Major .....48
Marche Funèbre .....50
Polacca Militaire .....52
Rondino in G Major .....54
Priere in E flat Major .....56
Nocturno in F Major .....57
Tyrolienne with Variations .....58
Romanza in C Major .....61
Rondo-Valse .....62
Danse des Montagnards .....65
Barcarole in F Major .....67
Tyrolienne in A Major .....69
Valse in D Major .....70
Siciliano in G Major .....72
Aria in F Major .....74
Polonaise in E Major .....76

# Twenty-Five Primary Etudes
Opus 166

## Etude No. 1 in C Major

HENRI BERTINI

Lento

Exercise

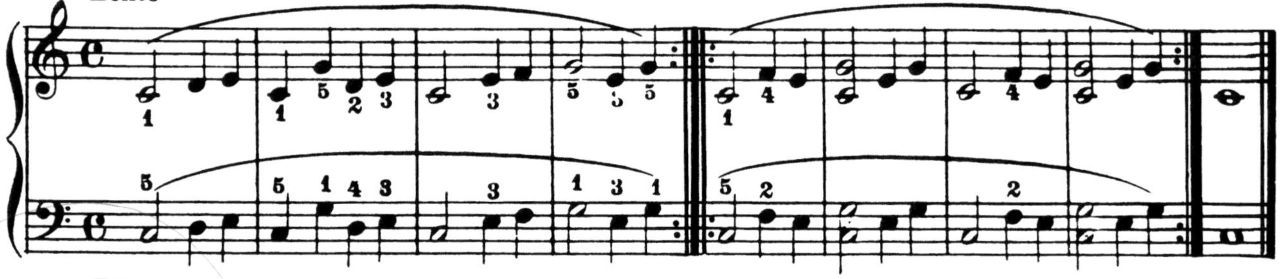

Allegretto

Prelude

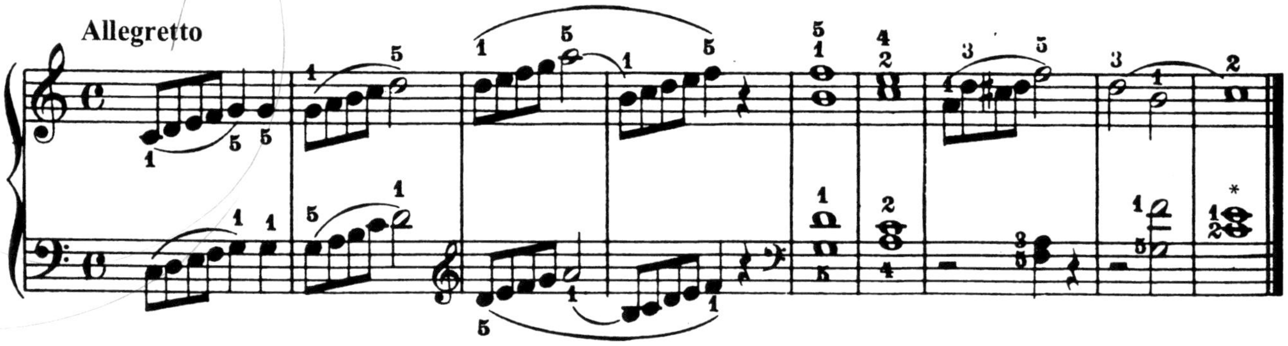

Lento

Etude

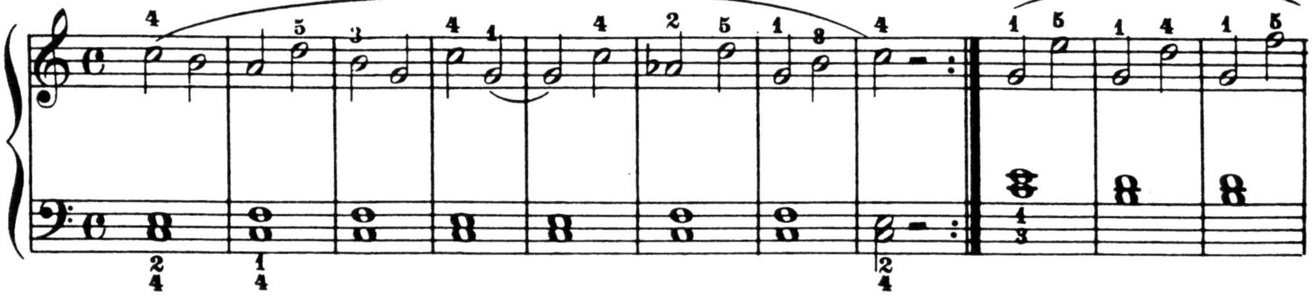

* In similar places $\frac{2}{3}$ for larger hands.

# Etude No. 2 in C Major

# Etude No. 3 in G Major

# Etude No. 4 in C Major

# Etude No. 5 in C Major

# Etude No. 6 in G Major

**Allegretto**

Exercise

**Lento**

Prelude

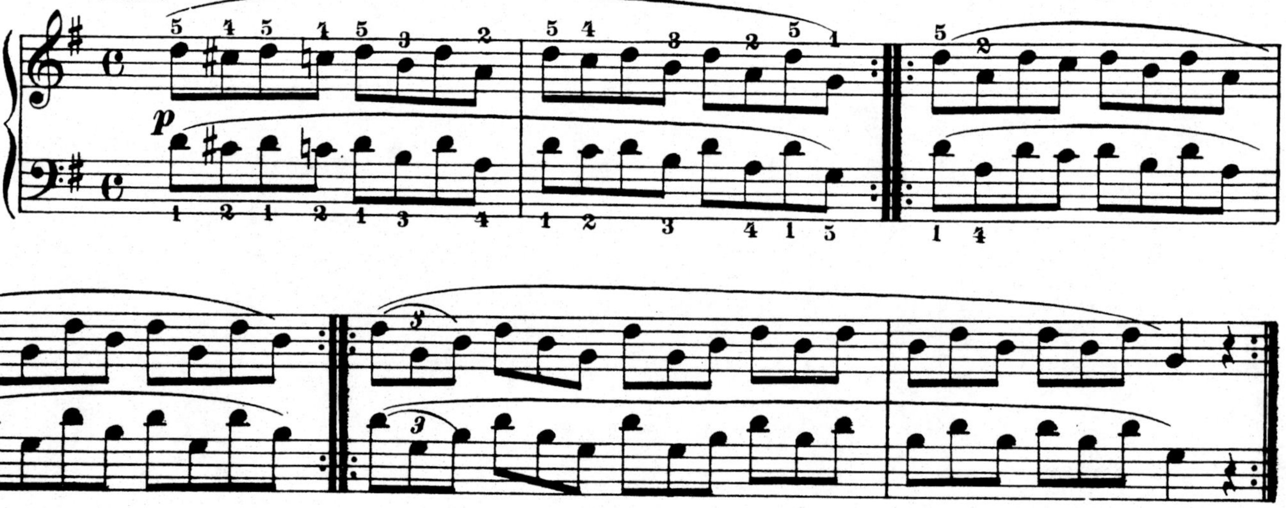

**Andante**

Etude

# Etude No. 7 in G Major

# Etude No. 8 in G Major

# Etude No. 9 in A Minor

Exercise

Prelude

Etude

# Etude No. 10 in G Major

# Etude No. 11 in D Major

# Etude No. 12 in F Major

# Etude No. 13 in C Major

# Etude No. 14 in A Major

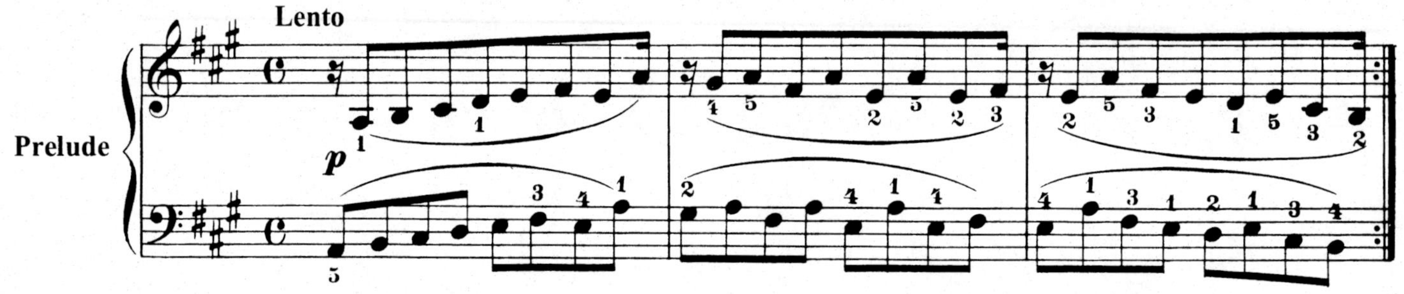

dimin.
p
cresc.
f
p
f
p
pp
cresc.
f

# Etude No. 15 in C Major

Andante quasi allegretto
Etude
p
cresc.
f
p
f

# Etude No. 16 in B Flat Major

**Allegro**

**Exercise**

**Allegro**

**Prelude**

**Allegretto**

**Etude**

a) Every note - group in this Prelude, and in the following Etude, for special practice, begins with the 3rd finger, although the 2nd is sometimes more convenient.

b) For further practice, every note - group may be begun with the 2nd or 4th finger.

simile

# Etude No. 17 in C Major

# Etude No. 18 in E Minor

# Etude No. 19 in D Major

# Etude No. 20 in C Minor

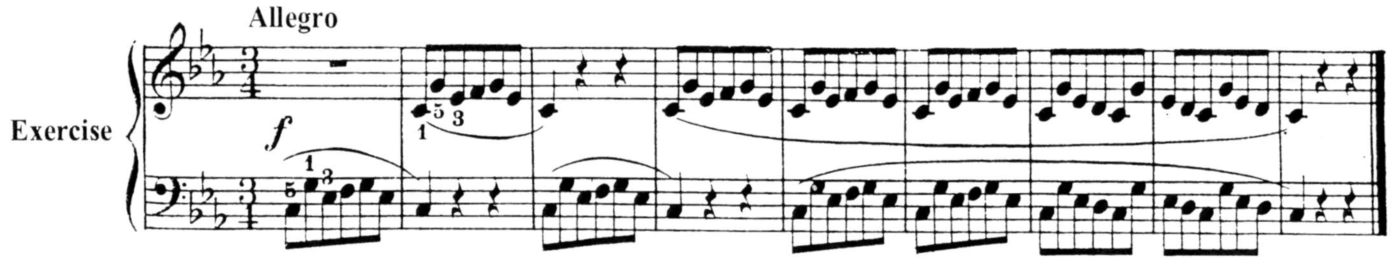


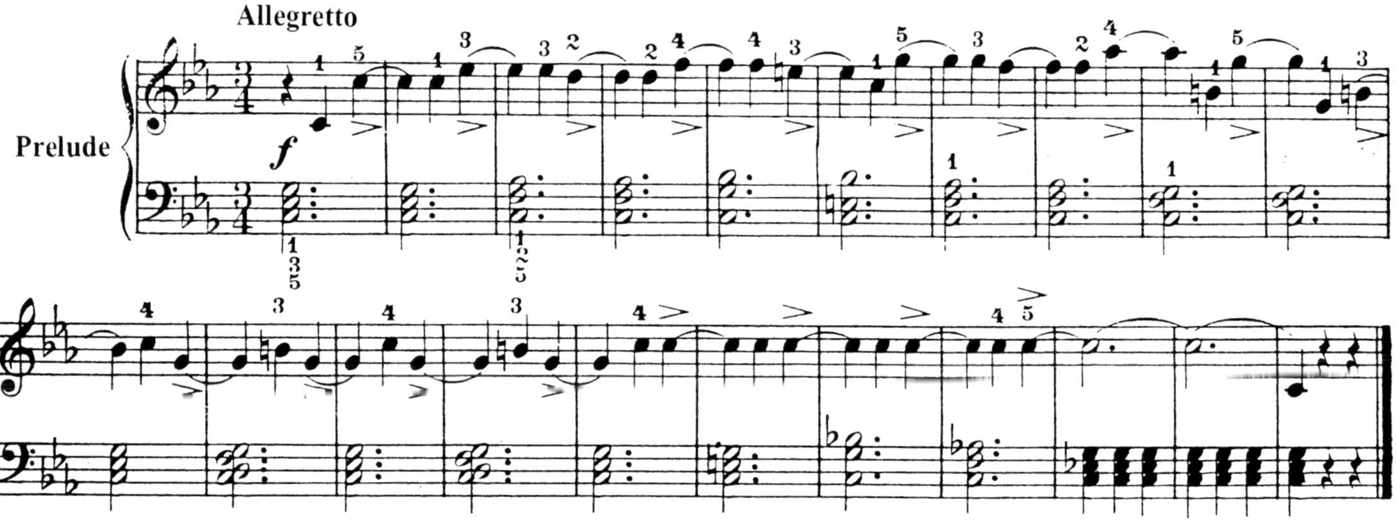

# Etude No. 21 in D Major

* Composer's fingering 2 for every eighth note.

*D.S. al Fine.*

# Etude No. 22 in E Minor

# Etude No. 23 in C Major

# Etude No. 24 in C Major

This page has been left blank to facilitate page turns.

# Etude No. 25 in E Flat Major

# Twenty-Four Etudes

Opus 101

## Valse in B Flat Major

HENRI BERTINI

# Conzonetta in A Minor

a tempo
p
Ped. Ped. Ped.
Ped. Ped.
pp
pp
pp
Ped.
ff
Ped.

# Rondino in F Major

**Allegretto moderato (♩ = 84)**

Fine
staccato
rall.
a tempo
D.S.

# Aria in A Major

dimin.
a tempo
rall.
p legato
Ped.
Ped.
Ped.
Ped.
Ped.
p
Ped.
pp
Ped.

# Minuet and Trio in E Minor

# Theme and Variations in E Minor

a tempo
p
rall.
f
Var. IV.
Più lento
p
f
dimin.
rall.
p
Var. V.
p a tempo
p
f
p
f
fz
p
Coda.
p
pp
estinto
rall.
pp

# Ballade in F Minor

# Marche in A Major

**Allegretto moderato (♩ = 126)**

33

# Adagio in F Major

**Adagio ma non troppo** (♩ = 84)

34

cresc.
f
ff
p
pp
rall.
a tempo
cresc
mf

# Marche Funèbre

**Lento maestoso (♩ = 104)**

f
pp
pp
pp
cresc.
f
p
fz
pp
pp

# Polacca Militaire

rall.
molto rall.
a tempo

# Rondino in G Major

**Andante grazioso (♪ = 108)**

37

rall.
piu lento
a tempo
p
pp
rall.
pp

# Prière in E Flat Major

# Nocturno in F Major

# Tyrolienne with Variations

f
p
sf
Adagio.
p
ff
p
rall.

più lento
f
dim.
Allegretto brillante
pp
pp
rall
a tempo
ff

# Romanza in C Major

**Andante quasi Adagio (♩ = 100)**

# Rondo - Valse

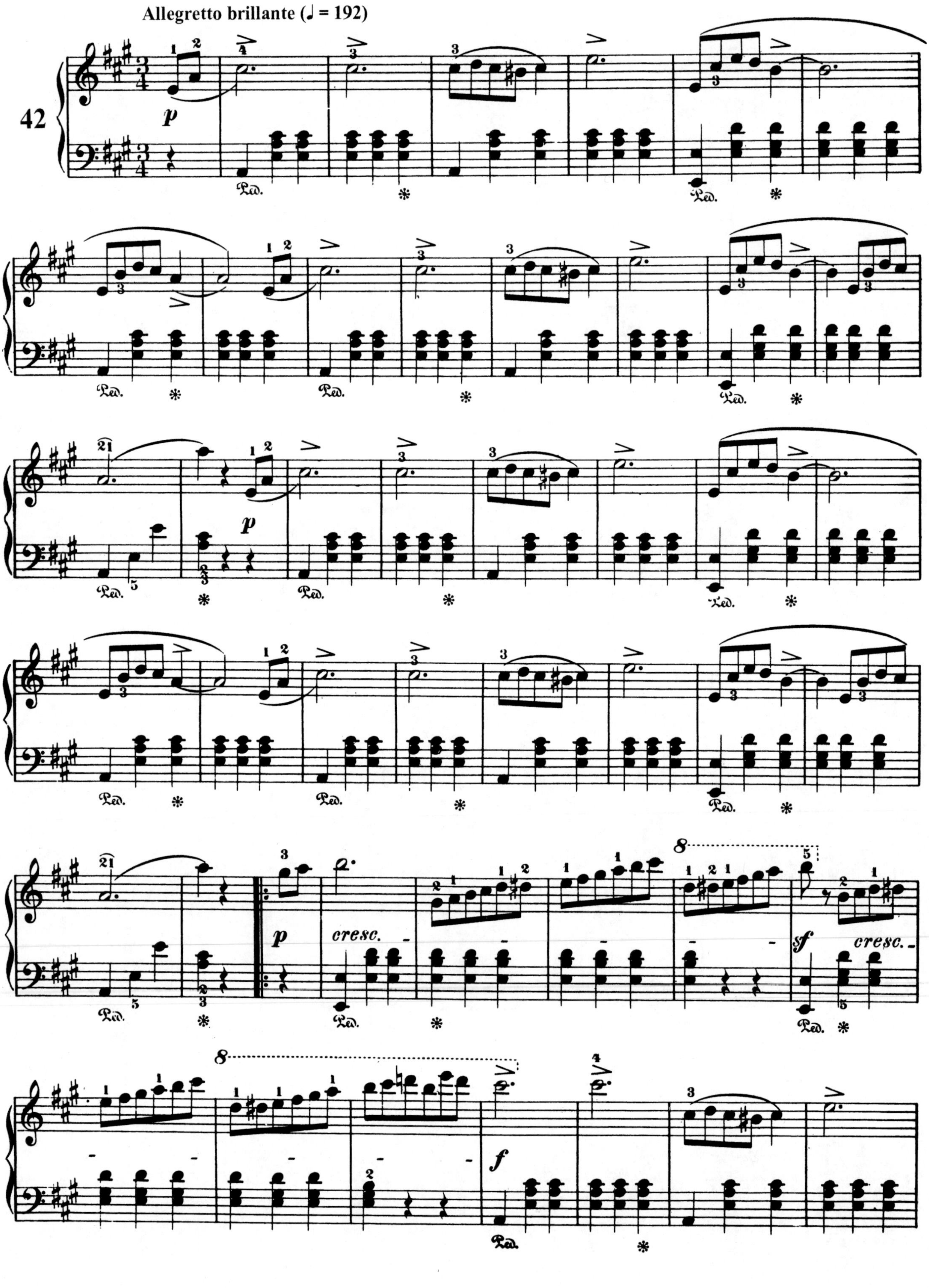
Allegretto brillante (♩ = 192)
42
p
cresc.
sf
f

risoluto
ff
p
ff
p
ff
p
p
cresc.

cresc.
poco più lento
rall.

# Danse des Nontagnards

legatissimo
pp
f
ff
molto rall.
ff a tempo
Ped.

# Barcarole in F Major

pp
rall.

# Tyrolienne in A Major

# Valse in D Major

p
f
cresc.
ff
Ped.

# Siciliano in G Major

a tempo
rall.
p
cresc.
rall. dimin.
a tempo
p
leggiero
p
più lento
pp
fz
pp

# Aria in F Major

**Andante (♩ = 108)**

cresc.
p
p
f
dimin.
cresc.
f
f
pp
f
p
p
pp

# Polonaise in E Major

**Allegretto quasi andante (♩ = 104)**

p
f
dimin.
pp rall.
a tempo
p
rall.
a tempo
p
leggiero
Ped.
pp
ff

Kalmus